The Book of African Names

Molefi Kete Asante

Africa World Press, Inc.
P.O. Box 1892
Trenton, New Jersey 08607

First Printing 1991

Cover, book design and production:
Ife Designs

Illustrations:
Chapters II thru V from *African Designs from Traditional Sources* by Geoffrey Williams
Chapter Openings by Ife Nii Owoo
Chapter VI by Barbara Nickens

Library of Congress Catalog Card Number: 91-72493

ISBN: 0-86543-254-6 Cloth
0-86543-255-4 Paper

The Book of African Names

Molefi Kete Asante

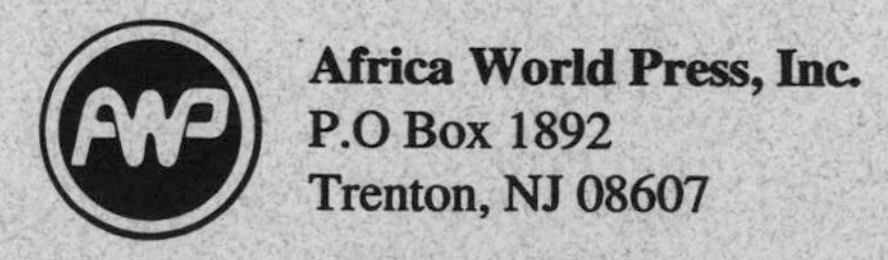

Africa World Press, Inc.
P.O Box 1892
Trenton, NJ 08607

Table of Contents

I. Introduction

I have long felt the need to write a naming book that was truly based upon an Afrocentric orientation to the world. This is not to say that we have not seen a great many African name books in the past. Unfortunately those books have often come with the peculiar baggage of their authors. Some of these books have been predominantly Ibo books, some primarily Yoruba books, and still others Islamic books, Swahili books, and so forth.

Name books, like other expression of a self-conscious people, must emerge from an Afrocentric perspective if they are to have currency for a Pan-African community. Otherwise they are merely the reflections of some person's esoteric interest in creating a name book. Although what I have said is correct, the attempt to develop name books is itself a response to a cultural need. African people recognize the need to have books that provide guidance in the important naming function.

Two Principles

The present book is based on two principles. First, the use of African names must be governed by an appreciation of African culture; and secondly, all African names are not necessarily positive for cultural and spiritual rebirth. The first principle is necessary because there are people who walk around with names like "Rhodesia" and "Muganda" because they chose African names without an Afrocentric guide. A mother in Buffalo, New York looked on an old map of Africa and saw the country of "Rhodesia" and named her daughter. Of course, Rhodesia was based on the name of Cecil John Rhodes, one of the worst racists of all time; it was not an African name. The country has since become Zimbabwe. The name "Muganda" in the Bajita language means something like being "half-baked," literally "Half full of water" or a "bundle of grass." A person seeking to rise above circumstances would have to be extremely lacking in sensitivity to name a child "Muganda." Yet there are African name books with this name in it.

Selection of Entries

The present book is severely selective. While this is the most comprehensive African name book to date, it omits some of the more negative names, such as names meaning "evil one," "sad," "trouble," and so forth. Anyone interested in such names may consult any African language dictionary or some of the older African name books. Names have also been chosen for their meaning to Africans in the diaspora as well as those on the continent. Choosing names with importance to a self-transforming people has required some slight changes in definition so that the names could be understood in their original intention. For example, the name "Oding" literally means "wood carver" but I have taken the liberty to say "sculptor" or "artist." Nowhere have I or would I change the substantive meaning of an African name.

Entries to this book came from many sources. The principal source has been from my African students at several universities and my own knowledge of lexical items in several African languages. In addition to what my students told me and what I know myself I have surveyed as many African name books as I possibly could to see what was missing and what was incorrectly interpreted. I have also found names in novels, poems, and short stories from Africa. This multi-faceted process of collecting names is important because most African name books concentrate on one ethnic or regional group. With entries from students I have managed to break the strangle-hold of a particular group or another. Nevertheless, since most

Africans in the Americas are from the West Coast (Mauretania to Angola) I have used more West African names. However, this book has more names from the other regions of Africa than any African name book before it.

A Pan-Africanist Approach

A special feature of this book is its Pan-African nature. You will notice that there is no reference to any particular ethnic group in the name list. You will also see that all the names of a region are grouped according to gender. This eliminates the problem, found in some books that list by ethnic groups, of having to find a female or male name by running down the entire list of all names grouped under "Yoruba." What I have also done is to impose a kind of Afrocentric unity over the regions and to say that ethnic groups is not more important than the name or the region. I believe the problem some people will have with this type of organization is that they will know what a name means but they will not have the "liberty" of saying that it means so and so in the Wolof, Ibo, or Twi language. I have deliberately taken away that "liberty" in order to suggest that we think more of ourselves as AFRICANS than any one ethnicity. By doing this we also insure that some of our names will take on a more universal recognition within the African world.

Naming is significant because it assists us in identifying who we are and where we think we should be going. Closely connected to the Umfundalai Ceremonies and other rites of change, the naming ceremony is sacred within the context of our history and experience. Each time parents name a child they are saying something about the way they want that child to be, about who they see themselves as, and about what the future of the African people should be. They may do this consciously or unconsciously but nevertheless the name goes with the child as a symbol of the people. To name an African child "Mary," "James," "Robert," "Mao," Ronald," "Arthur," "Carol," "Donald," "Betty," or "Sarah" is to introduce a particular cultural message into the family. Names do have meaning. When you meet Dr. Maulana Karenga and you greet him, "Hello, Maulana" you are saying "Hello, Master Teacher."

Those who see me and say "Molefi" are saying "Keeper of the Traditions." When I call to my wife whose name is "Kariamu, please come here" I am saying with great respect "One who reflects the Almighty, please come here."

Changing Names

Since many of us born in the Americas possess names given to us by slave owners or taken from the names of our former slave masters it is fitting that we should decide to choose for ourselves those names that best reflect our history and culture. It is certainly an easy matter to see how names were at one time chosen because we had no knowledge of Africa or little knowledge of our heritage. But now that we have become knowledgeable of our African past, we know our history, and we are proud of the struggles of our ancestors, we must correct the errors that occurred when our people were as Malcolm X used to say, "deaf and dumb."

To change your slave name to an African name is technically a simple matter but one that requires thought and reflection. The technical or legal aspect of it is the easiest part of thc whole process. You simply go to a lawyer and tell him that you want to change your name. He will quote you a fee, normally not very expensive as legal fees go, and begin the process of changing all of your records to reflect the name change. In most cases you will not have to make an appearance in court. The lawyer will appear for you and enter the necessary papers. You will receive a court document stating which court, the date, the country and the location of your name change. I carried a small xeroxed copy of my legal name change with me for a few months in case someone questioned my name. Soon this became unnecessary.

There is nothing wrong with consulting with leading Afrocentricists, male or female, who have changed their names. They can often help you in choosing a name that fits you. You may even want to have a private naming ceremony for yourself. This is definitely in keeping with the best tradition of consciousness.

I have written this book for the children as much as for ourselves to give them a chance to become all that their names will suggest. The research, time, and effort that have gone into this book will be repaid by the studious, serious manner in which you, the user, apply yourself to the regaining of our senses.

The Significance of Names

In ancient Africa, beginning in Nubia and Kemet (Egypt) thousands of years ago, every boy and every girl was given a name according to significance. A boy, for example, had to learn how to do certain things, would be initiated into the religion of the ancestors and certain professions. A girl, for example, would master knowledge of agriculture and the behavior of children. This means that information from the family tradition would have been passed to the children. It goes without saying that these practices are found in some other cultures, notable are the English where one finds Smith, Fowler, Hunter, Mason, Carpenter, Turner, and Baker as names. Today, of course, those names may be held by people who are no longer in those professions.

Names are also important because they may affect a person's behavior. However, as the story in Essence Magazine by Kariamu Welsh, *She was Linda before she was Ayesha,* clearly testifies, names ought to mean something today. I believe that the proper name for a child has a psychological effect on her or him. Since names are designations for the sum total of the person, it is important to make the right choice. Parents or guardians should also give children African names before they are presented for rites of passage. This marks for the child who does not have an African name the significance of the ceremony associated with the rites of passage. Since behavior and attitude are tied directly to a person's sense of self esteem and importance, the choice of name should not be left to chance or simply drawn from a lottery, it should be well thought out, discussed, and then decided upon.

This book should prove to be a major asset to the contemporary family seeking to find the proper name for children or for adults who would like to dispense with their slave names and secure a proper African name.

II. Southern Region

Female	Meaning
Boniswa	This has been revealed
Chenzira	Born while parents were travelling
Chioneso	She is a guiding light
Chipo	What a great gift
Chuma	Beads are not richer than we are
Inaambura	Mother of the rains
Linda	Wait for goodness
Lindiwe	We have waited for joy
Magano	She is a gift
Maideyi	What did you expect
Mashama	This is a surprise
Mbakondja	I have struggled
Muchaneta	Perhaps you will get tired
Mudiwa	This one is truly loved

Ndapewa	I have been given this one
Nobantu	Will be loved by people
Nocawe	She was born on Sunday
Nokhwezi	This is a morning star
Nomabaso	A welcomed present
Nomatha	A real surprise
Nobini	I now have two girls
Nombulelo	I give thanks
Nompumelelo	We have success
Nomsa	Kindness is found
Nomthandazo	We prayed to the ancestors
Nomusa	This is mercy
Nondudumo	The time was thunderous
Nondummiso	We give her praises
Nonggawuse	Send falsehood away
Nonkululeko	Freedom is here
Nontando	Full of love
Nontiupheko	Suffering is over
Nontobeko	Meekness comes now
Nontothuzelo	She will console us
Nonzwakazi	This is beauty
Nonzenzele	She will do it herself
Nozibele	She is a generous one
Nozipho	This is a gift
Noxolo	Peaceful
Ntathu	I have three girls
Ntombentle	A lovely girl
Ntombizine	The fourth girl
Ntombizodwa	All are girls

Pepukayi	We are awake
Pumla	Now we can rest
Ripuree	Think about this
Rudo	Love
Rufaro	Happiness
Runako	Beauty

Sakile	Peace and beauty
Sekayi	Happy with laughter
Sibongile	Thanks
Sibusiso	Blessing
Sihle	Beautiful
Sikhumbuzo	Reminder
Sikose	This is tradition
Sipo	A gift
Sithabile	We are happy
Spiwe	We were given

Thandiwe	Beloved
Thembeka	Trustworthy is her name
Thokozile	Happiness
Uvatera	God help us
Vuyelwa	Joy
Vuyisa	Made happy
Zenzele	She will do it herself
Zine	I have four girls

Male	Meaning
Ayzize	Let it come
Banga	Sharp as a knife
Bekitemba	One you can trust
Betserai	Sent to help out
Bongani	Sing with joy
Diliza	Destroyer of evil
Dingane	One in time of need
Dumisani	Herald of the future
Gaika	Gifted in sculpture
Gamba	He is a warrior
Homaleni	Take up arms and defend self
Hondo	One who is prepared for war
Inaani	Who is left at home?

Jongilanga	He faces the sun
Kazandu	You are a young man
Kokayi	Call the people to hear
Landuleni	One who finds greatness
Langalibalele	Sun is shining
Mahluli	This is a victor
Mangwiro	The enlightened one
Mapfumo	The soldier
Matsimela	The roots are firm
Mbonisi	One who will teach us
Molefi	He keeps Traditions

Momar	This one is a philosopher
Moyo	Heart; ancient totem of Rozvi kings
Muata	He searchs for truth
Mtheto	One who loves law
Mthinklulu	As strong as a tree
Mthunzi	This one is thunderous
Mxali	Anxiety is over
Mxolisi	Peacemaker

Ndabeexinhle	This is good news
Ndoro	A shell/emblem of kingship
Ndumiso	Praise follows this one
Njabulo	Happiness
Nkokheli	He is a leader
Nkosi	He will rule
Nkululeko	Freedom is ours
Ntsikelelo	Blessing
Nyandoro	He wears the crown
Nyenyedzi	Star
Nyikadzino	This land belongs to us
Rikondja	Our nation is struggling

Shumba	Lion
Sigidi	He is like a thousand
Sikumbuzo	The ancestors remind us
Simangaliso	He came quickly
Simba	Strength
Sipho	A gift
Siyolo	This is joy
Solwazi	He is knowledge
Sondai	Keep pushing forward
Sondisa	Bring him near to us
Tagulani	Be happy
Takadiyi	How are we doing
Tangeni	Let us give praise
Tapfuma	We are wealthy
Taruvinga	We have come for it
Tichawoma	We shall see

III. Central Region

Female	**Meaning**
Adero	She gives life
Dyese	This is my fortune
Kafi	Serene
Katokwe	Happiness is mine
Kemba	She is full of faith
Kilolo	Youth shines on her
Lumengo	A flower of the people
Mawakana	I yield to the ancestors
Migozo	She is earnest
Nakpangi	This one is a star
Nalungo	She is beautiful
Nataki	She is of royal birth

Ndunba	We are happy
Ndunga	She will be famous
Niambi	The melody is heard
Nkenge	She is brilliant
Nsombi	Abounding joy
Nzinga	She is beauty and courage

Male	**Meaning**
Cazembe	He is a wise man
Changa	Strong as iron
Changamire	He is as the sun
Diop	Ruler, scholar

Dunduza	He will venture to see
Jawanza	This one is dependable
Kakuyon	He arms the people
Kalonji	He will be victorious
Lasana	A poet of the people
Lumumba	Gifted, brilliant
Mani	He came from the mountain
Mpyama	He shall inherit
Mugabe	Intelligent, quick
Mutope	Protector
Mwanze	The child is protected
Mwata	We have been sensible

Nogomo	He will be prosperous
Nyahuma	A helper of others
Oronde	Appointed
Sanga	He came from the valley
Sokoni	He came from the sea
Tacuma	He is alert
Yamro	This one is courteous
Yero	A born soldier
Yerodin	He is studious

IV. The Eastern Region

Female	Meaning
Adong	No father was present
Aisha	She is life
Amina	She is trustworthy
Andaiye	A daughter comes home
Asha	She is life
Ashia	Life
Asura	Born during month of Ashur
Asya	Overcomes by grief
Ayan	Bright
Ayanna	This is a beautiful flower
Aziza	The child is gorgeous
Bahati	My fortune is good

Chausiku	Born at night
Chuike	She brings peace in time of trouble
Daib	She is excellent
Dalila	Gentleness is her soul
Damamli	A beautiful vision

Deiriai	Child of the dry season
Deka	She who satisfies
Ewunike	Like a fragrance
Fujo	She brings wholeness
Gulai	Born between the rainy seasons

Habiba	The beloved
Hasina	She is good
Jaha	This is dignity
Jemila	Beautiful
Kalifa	Holy child
Kariamu	One who reflects the almighty
Kenyetta	She is beautiful music
Kesi	Born when father worked hard

Khatiti	Sweet little thing
Layla	Born at night
Lulu	She is a pearl
Maulidi	Born during the month of Maulidi
Micere	
Mijiza	Works with her hands

Mosi	She is the first born
Muga	Mother of all
Mukumtagara	Born in the time of war
Mukumutara	Born during the time of Mutara
Nadifa	She was born between the seasons
Nafula	It was raining
Najuma	She abounds in joy

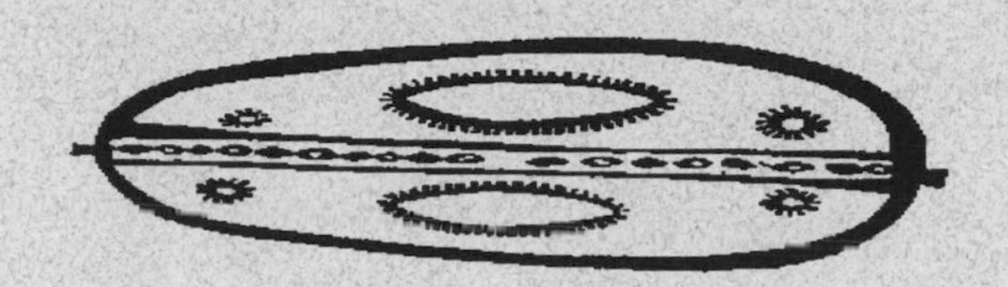

Njeri	Daughter of a warrior
Ngena	Majestic in service
Ngina	One sho serves
Pili	The second child
Rhamah	My sweetness
Sala	Gentle

Shamfa	Sunshine
Uwingabiye	Sent by the deity
Wambui	Singer of songs

Male	Meaning
Abeid	He is a leader
Alimayu	God is honored
Ato	This one is brilliant
Ayele	Powerful
Babu	A doctor
Bhoke	He wanders the land
Bomani	A mighty soldier
Cacanja	A medicine priest
Dedan	He loves the city

Male	Meaning
Erasto	A man of peace
Idi	Born during the Idi festival
Jaramogi	He travels often
Jojo	This one is a story teller
Kagale	Born in the time of trouble
Kahero	Born at home

Male	Meaning
Kamau	Quiet soldier
Kambui	Fearless
Karanja	A guide
Karume	He protects the land and forest
Kassahun	To compensate for
Kenyatta	A musician
Ketema	He comes from the valley
Kiambu	This one will be rich
Kimani	Sailor

Macharia	An eternal friend
Machumu	Blacksmith
Makonnen	Ruler
Mbiyu	This one runs fast
Mganga	A doctor
Mombera	He loves adventure
Mugeta	One born at night
Mugo	A wise person
Mwando	An efficient worker
Mwangi	He will have many children

Nadif	Born between two seasons
Ngugi	The traditions are set
Njonjo	Disciplined
Oboi	The second son
Odai	The third son
Oding	An artist
Oginga	One who drums
Okang	The first son
Sentwaki	There is courage in him

Walialu	He makes thing return
Wimana	He belongs to the deity
Yusufu	This one charms

V. The Western Region

Female	**Meaning**
Aba	Born on Thursday
Abebi	We asked and got her
Abebja	Born at a time of grief
Abeje	We asked for this one
Abena	Born on Tuesday
Abeo	Come to bring happiness
Abimbola	Born rich
Abia	Born on Tuesday
Ada	First daughter
Adaego	Daughter of wealth
Adaeke	Born on "Eke" market day
Adaeze	Princess
Adande	The challenger
Adanma	Daughter of beauty
Adanna	Father's daughter
Adanne	Mother's daughter
Adaoha	Daughter of the people

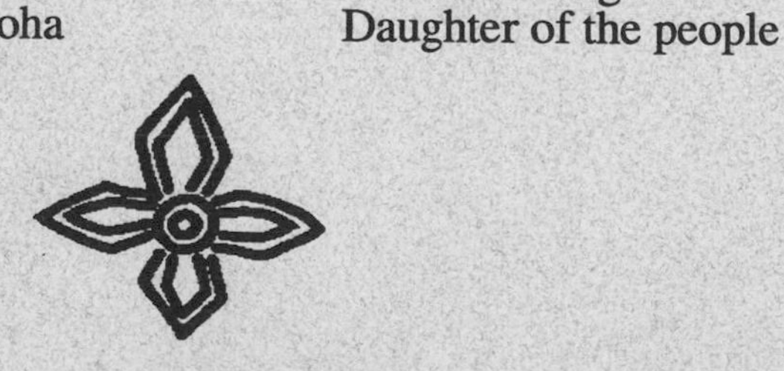

Adebomi	Crown had covered my nakedness
Adedagbo	Happiness is crown
Adedewe	The crown is shattered
Adedoja	Crown is worthy
Adeleke	Crown brings happiness
Adeola	Crown brings honor
Adiagha	First daughter
Adjua	Born on Monday
Aduke	Much loved
Adwin	Artist
Adzo	Born on Monday
Afafa	First child of second husband
Afam	Friendly
Afi	Born on Friday
Afryea	Born during happy times
Agbeko	Life
Agodichinma	As it pleases God
Ahuzuomoke	May I be perfectly well
Aidoo	Arrived

Aisha	Life
Aiyetoro	Peace on earth
Akanika	Born during the harmattan
Akenke	To want her is to love her
Akili	Wisdom
Akuabia	Here is wealth
Akuako	Younger of twins
Akwate	Elder of twins
Alaba	Born after Idowu

Aladinma	I am happy with my stay
Alaezi	I am exonerated
Alili	She weeps
Aluma	Come here
Ama	Born on Saturday
Amadi	Dedicated to "Amadi"
Amanchechi	Who knows God's will
Amaogechukwu	No one knows God's time
Amauzo	Who knows the way
Ambe	We begged God for it
Amevi	Child of a human being
Amonke	To know her is to pet her
Anan	Fourth born
Anuli	Joy
Arusi	Born during wedding
Asabi	Of select birth
Asesimba	Noble birth
Asha	Life
Asong	Seventh born
Atsufi	Born twin
Ayah	Bright
Ayo	Joy
Ayobami	I am blessed with joy
Ayobunmi	Joy is given to me
Ayodele	Joy comes home
Ayofemi	Joy like me
Ayoluwa	Joy of our people
Ayoola	Joy in wealth
Aziza	Goregous
Azuka	Support is paramount

Banasa	Born on Monday
Binta	Beautiful daughter
Bolanile	The wealth of this house
Borishade	She respects the deities
Bunmi	My gift
Bupe	Hospitality
Buruku	Named after the deity “Buruku”
Camara	One who teaches from experience
Charakupa	That which you are given
Chausiku	Born at night
Chiamaka	“Chi” is spendid
Chidi	“Chi” exists
Chijioke	“Chi” owns gifts
Chika	“Chi” is supreme
Chiku	Chatterer
Chinasaokuru	God answers for me

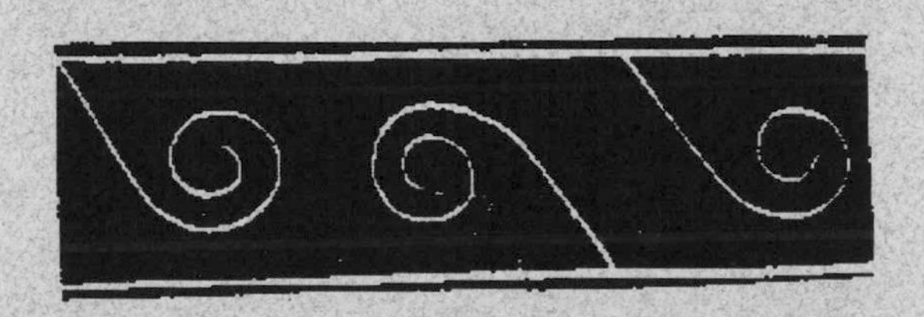

Chinenye	“Chi” gives
Chinwe	It belongs to God
Chinyere	God is the giver
Chipo	Gift
Chizoba	May “Chi” protect
Dada	Child with curly hair
Daib	Excellent
Dalia	Gentle
Dalmar	Versatile
Dayo	Joy arrives

Deka	She who pleases
Doto	Second of twins
Dridzienyo	Birth is good
Dzidodo	Sued to suffering
Dzidzo	Happiness
Dzigbodi	Patience

Ebere	Mercy
Ebun	Gift
Echijiole	What has tomorrow in store?
Edem	Dedicated to the God Ndem
Efioanwan	Born on the market day "Ofiong"
Efua	Born on Friday
Eka	Mother of the earth
Ekanem	Mother of All
Ekechi	God's creation
Ekedinna	Eke is good
Elewechi	We await God
Elon	God loves me
Enam	God gave it to me
Enomwoyi	One who has graceEnyo
Enyo	It is enough for me

Enyonyam	It is good for me
Eshe	Life
Esi	Born on Sunday
Esinam	God has heard me
Ezigbo	Beloved

Fabayo	A lucky birth is joy
Fayola	Good fortune
Feechi	Worship God

Fola	Honor
Folade	Honor arrives
Foluke	Placed in God's care
Fujo	Born after parent's departure
Fumiya	Suffering
Fuvi	A child born into suffering
Ginikanwa	What is more precious than a child?
Guedado	Wanted by no one
Gulai	Born between the monsoon season
Habibka	Sweetheart

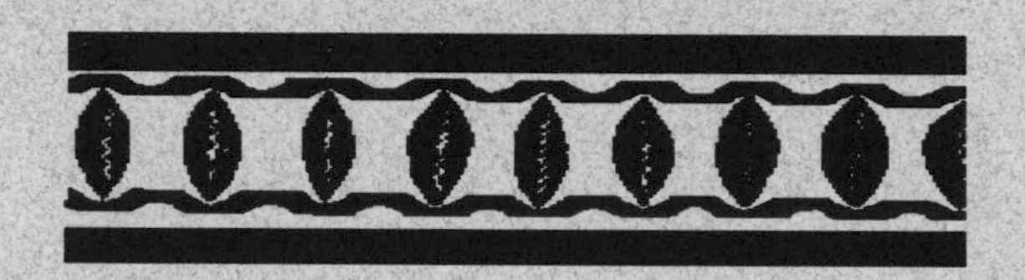

Hadiya	Gift
Halina	Gentle
Haomyaro	Born during conflicts
Hasina	Good
Hembadon	The winner
Idowu	First child after twins
Idomenyin	Hope
Ife	Lover of art and culture
Ige	Born feet first
Iheoma	A welcome child
Iheyinwa	All comes through Divine Providence
Ihuoma	Good luck; lucky child
Ijeoma	A good journey

Ijoma	Travel Safely
Ikusegham	Peace is better than war
Isoke	A satisfying gift from God
Iyabo	Mother has come back
Izebe	Long expected child

Jaha	Dignity
Jamila	Beautiful
Jumoke	Everyone loves the child
Jwahir	The golden woman
Kadija	The prophet's wife
Kai	Lovable
Kamania	Like the moon
Kamba	Tortoise
Kansiwa	The poor
Karamoko	Studious
Kelinde	Second born of twins

Kesi	Born when father had difficulties
Khoranhlai	She who brings sun
Kokumo	This one will not die again
Koliraga	Weeping
Kumiwa	Brave
Laraba	Wednesday
Layia	Born at night
Lebechi	Watch God

Limbe	Joyfulness
Lololi	There is always love
Lolonyo	Love is beautiful
Lolovivi	There's always love
Lozokun	Forget quarrel
Lulu	Precious

Mariama	Gift of God
Malene	Tower
Manana	Lustrous
Marka	Steady rain
Masani	Has gap between teeth
Masika	Born during rainy season
Maudisa	Sweet
Mawasi	In God's hands
Mayinuna	Expressive
Mgbafor	Born on Afor market day
Mgbeke	Born on Eke market day
Mgbeorie	Born on Orie market day
Mkiwa	Orphan
Mwa	Beauty
Modupe	I'm grateful (to God)
Moriba	Curious
Mudiwa	Beloved
Mukamutara	Mutara's daughter
Mukamtagara	Born in time of war

Nabinye	Producer of twins
Nabulungi	Beautiful one
Nafula	Born during rainy season
Nafuma	Born feet first
Naliaka	Wedding
Nalo	Much loved
Nalongo	Mothers of twins
Namono	Younger of twins
Nana	Mother of the earth
Nangleni	Fish
Nasike	Born in the locust season
Nayo	We have joy
Neema	Born during prosperous times
Ngozi	Blessing
Nini	Strong as stone; industrious one
Njemile	Upstanding
Njeri	Anointed
Njideka	Survival is paramount
Nkechi	Loyal
Nkechinyere	Whichever God gives
Nkeka	Tenderness
Nne	Mother
Nnennaya	Her father's mother
Nobuhle	Beauty
Noni	Gift of God

Nonyameko	Patience
Nombese	A wonderful child
Nwabugwu	A child is the parent's honor
Nwabundozi	A child is a blessing
Nwadighu	A child is a thing of beauty
Nwadimkpa	A child is important
Nwadinobi	A child is dear
Nwadiuko	A child is scarce

Nwajindu	A child sustains life
Nwakaegbo	A child is more valuable than money
Nwamaka	A child is so beautiful
Nwanneka	Brotherhood is better
Nwaoma	A beautiful child
Nwanyioma	A beautiful lady
Nwugo	Like eagle
Nyahkomago	Second child after twin
Nyiramohoro	Peaceful
Oare	Saintly
Obiagaeliaku	She has come to enjoy
Obianuju	Born at the time of plenty
Obioma	Kindhearted
Ode	Born along the road

Oji	Giftbearer
Okolo	Friendly
Olabisi	Joy is multiplied
Olabunmi	Honor has rewarded me
Olunfunke	God gives me to care for
Olufunmilayo	God gives me joy
Oluremi	God consoles me
Omolara	Born at the right time
Omorose	Beautiful child
Omosede	A child is more than a king
Omosupe	A child is supreme
Onyema	Sorrow

Oraefo	Affectionate
Oseye	The happy one
Ozibodi	Patience
Ozioma	Good news
Panya	A twin child
Pili	The second born
Ramia	Prophet
Raohiya	Agreeable
Rasida	Righteous
Raziya	Agreeable, sweet

Rehema	Comparison
Rufano	Happiness
Saada	Help

Male	Meaning
Abanobi	There's no entrance to the mind
Abaronye	Whom are you threatening?
Abasi	Stern
Abayomi	God saved me from derision
Abeeku	Born on Wednesday
Abegunde	Born during the Egungun festival
Abena	Pure
Abi	To guard
Abiade	Born of royal parents
Abimbola	Born rich
Abiodun	Born at the time of a festival
Abiola	Child born during first of the New Year
Abioye	Born during coronation
Abosi	Life plant
Abubakar	Noble
Abu	Nobility
Acholam	Do not provoke me
Achufusi	Do not reject

Male	Meaning
Adama	Majestic
Addae	Morning sun
Ade	Crown
Adebayo	He came in a joyful time
Adelaja	A crown is added to my wealth
Adika	First child of a second husband
Adisa	One who makes himself clear
Adjua	Noble
Afi	Spiritual
Afiba	By the sea

Agu	Lion
Ahoto	Peace
Ahonya	Prosperity
Ahurole	Loving
Aiyetoro	Peace on earth
Ajala	Dedicated to the God "Ala"
Ajayi	Born face downwards
Ajene	True
Ajuluchukwu	Asked of God
Akabueze	Support is paramount
Akamafula	May my work be rewarded
Akinlabi	We've born a brave child
Akintunde	A bravery man has come
Akinwunmi	I like bravery man
Ako	The first child
Akobundu	Purdence is life
Akna	Born on Thursday
Akua	Swcct messenger
Akwete	Younger of twins
Alaba	Born after Idowu
Ama	Happy
Ambe	We begged God for it

Amadi	Dedicated to the God Amadi
Amaechi	Who knows the future?
Amanambu	You can't tell from the start
Amatefe	Born after father's death
Amazu	Can't know everything
Ambakisye	God is merciful to me
Aminata	Good character
Amma	Famous
Ampah	Trust is supreme
Anapa	Morning

Anika	Goodness
Ankoma	Last born of parents
Ano	The second child
Anyanwu	Dedicated to the God
Asa	The third child
Ashaki	Beautiful
Assitou	Careful
Ata	Twin
Atakpa	If you eat me you'll die
Atiba	Understanding
Atsu	Younger of twins
Atu	Born on Saturday
Atuegbu	Fearless
Ayeola	Rainbow
Ayinde	He came after our praises
Ayo	Joy
Azagba	Born out of town

Azikiwe	Healthy
Azubuike	Support is strength

Baako	First born
Babafemi	Father loves me
Babatu	Peace maker
Babatunde	Father comes again Babu Willing
Baderinwa	Worthy of respect
Badru	Born at full moon
Badu	Tenth born
Bahati	Luck

Balogun	The chief (lord) of war
Bandele	Follow me home
Bangababo	Discord in the family
Baye	Straightforward
Bayo	There is joy
Bejide	Born during rainy season
Beluchi	Provided God approves
Beluonwu	Provided death does not overtake us
Birago	Down-to-earth, sensible
Bisa	Greatly loved
Bobo	Be humble
Bolewa	Happiness
Bosede	Born on Sunday
Bunwi	My gift
Butu	Weary
Bwerani	Welcome

Camara	Teacher
Chatha	An ending
Chatuluka	A departure
Chenzira	Born on the road
Chiamaka	God is splendid
Chibale	Kingship

Chicha	Beloved
Chidi	God exists
Chidubem	May God lead me
Chiemeka	God has done much
Chiganu	Hound
Chijioke	God owns gifts
Chikezie	May God create well
Chikozi	The reck
Chikwendu	Life depends on God
Chimanga	Maize
Chinangwa	Cassava
Chinouyazura	Will return
Chinyelu	Invincible
Chuma	God knows
Chuma	Wealth or rosary

Dada	A child with curly hair
Damani	Thoughtful
Danjuma	Born on Friday
Danladi	Born on Sunday
Dia	Champion
Diallo	Bold
Diarra	Gift

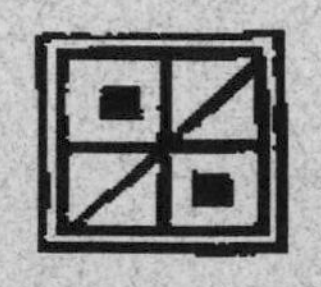

Dibia	Healer
Diji	Farmer
Dike	Warrior, brave
Djenaba	Affectionate
Donkor	A humble person
Duguma	Sharp as a spear
Dukuzumurenyi	Praise to God
Dumisani	Herald of truth
Durojaiye	Wait and enjoy the word
Duruji	Farmer
Eberechukwu	God's mercy
Ede	Sweetness
Edo	Love
Efuru	Daughter of heaven
Ehiozc	Above people's jealousy
Eintou	Pearl
Ejiikeme	Do not use force

Ekeama	Nature is splendid
Ekechukwu	God's creation
Ekejiuba	God owns wealth
Ekundayo	Sorrow has turned to happiness
Ekwutosi	Do not speak evil against others
Emenike	Do not use force
Enobakhare	What the chief says
Enomwoyi	One who has grace, charm
Ewansika	Secrets are not for sale
Eze	King
Ezeamaka	King is splendid
Ezenachi	The king rules
Ezeoha	The people's king

Fanta	Beautiful day
Faraji	Consolation
Fati	Robust
Fatou Mata	Beloved by all
Febechi	Worship God
Femi	Love me
Fenuku	Born after twins

Gamba	Warrior
Gavivi	Money is good
Ginikanwa	What is more valuable than a child?
Gogo	Like grandfather
Gowon	Rainmaker
Hawanya	A tear
Habimama	God exists

Hakizimana	Born on Thursday
Hondo	War
Ibeamaka	The agnates are splendid
Ibeawuchi	The agnates are not good

Ibrahim	Father is exalted
Idowu	Born after twins
Idrissa	Immortal
Ifeanacho	The desired child
Ifeanyichukwu	Nothing is impossible with God
Ifoma	Lasting friend
Ihechukwu	Light of God
Ikechukwu	The power of God
Ikenna	Father's power
Imarogbe	Born into a good family
Iroawuchi	Enmity is not "Chi"
Italo	Full of valor
Iwegbolu	May anger ceasc
Iwuchukwu	God's commandment

Jabari	Brave
Jabulani	Be happy
Jahi	Dignity
Jaja	God's gift
Jela	Father in pain at birth
Jojo	Born on Monday

Kafele	Worth dying for
Kamau	Quiet warrior
Kamdibe	Let me endure
Kampihe	God and see
Kamulira	Lamentable
Kamuzu	Medicinal
Kandia	Fortress
Kashka	Friendly

Kasimu	Keeper of the forest
Kasiya	Departure
Kayode	He brought joy
Keambirowo	Heap of blackness
Keanjaho	Heap of beans
Keanyandaarwa	Heap of beans
Kehnide	Twin who comes second
Keita	Worshipper
Kelechi	Thank God
Khamadi	Born on Thursday
Khari	Kingly
Kobla	Born on Tuesday
Kodjo	Born on Monday
Koffi	Born on Friday
Kojo	Unconquerable

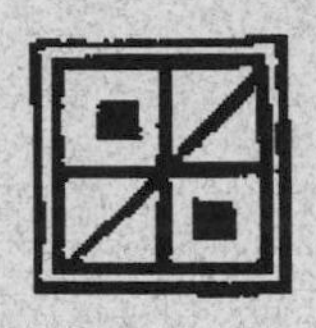

Konata	Man of high station
Kontar	An only child
Kufere	Do not forget
Kunle	Home is full with honors
Kwabena	Born on Tuesday
Kwacha	Morning
Kwaku	Born on Wednesday
Kwami	Born on Saturday
Kwasi	Born on Sunday
Kwende	Let us go
Kwesi	Conquering strength
Ligongo	Who is this?
Lisimba	Torn

Lizwelicha	New country
Lotachukwu	Remember God
Lumo	Born face downards
Mablevi	Don't deceive
Machupa	One who likes to drink
Madaadi	An age group
Madu	Man
Maduabuchi	Man is not God
Madubuike	Man is mother's strength
Madzimoyo	Water of life
Mahluli	Victor
Maidei	What did you want?
Makutano	Born in a meeting place
Malawa	Flowers
Mamboleo	Temporary
Masamba	Leaves
Masibuwa	Modern days
Maskini	Poor
Matunde	Fruits
Mawali	There is a God
Mawulode	God will provide
Mawulolo	God is great
Mbwana	Master
Mensa	Third son
Modeira	Teacher
Modibo	Helper
Modupe	Thank you (God)
Mongo	Famous

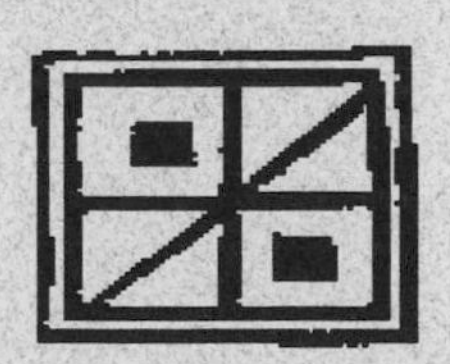

Montsho	Black
Mosi	First Born
Moyo	God health
Moyo	Heart
Mpasa	Mat
Mpumelelo	Success
Mwai	Good fortune
Mwita	The caller

Nabate	Little
Nadif	Born between the two seasons
Nakisisa	Child of the shadows
Nantambu	Man of destiny
Nassor	Victorious
Ndale	Trick
Ndubia	May life come
Ndubuisi	Life is the first thing
Nduka	Life is supreme
Ndukwe	If life permits

Ndulu	Dove
Ngoli	Happiness
Ngozi	Blessing
Ngunda	Dove
Niamke	God's gift
Nkandinshuti	I like friends
Nkcmdirim	Let mine be with me
Nkemefula	Let me not lose mine
Nkosi	Ruler
Nkpume	Solid as rock
Nkruma	Ninth born

Nnabugwu	Father is honor
Nnaemeka	Father has done much
N'namdi	Worthy
Nnamdi	My father is alive
Nolizwe	County
Nonyelum	Abide with me
Nosakhene	God's way is the only way
Nosiike	Be firm
Nuru	Born during daylight
Nwabudike	Child is power
Nwachukwu	God's child

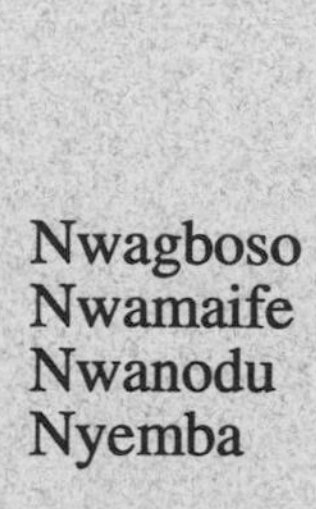

Nwagboso	A child does not run
Nwamaife	An intelligent child
Nwanodu	May the child survive
Nyemba	Beans

Oba	King
Obadele	The king comes home
Obafemi	The king likes me
Obaseki	The Oba surpasses the market
Obiajulu	The heart is consoled
Obiajunwa	The heart does not reject
Obialo	The heart is comforted
Obianuria	The heart is happy
Obinna	Dear to the father
Obinwanne	Dear to the brother
Obinwoke	Manly heart
Ochi	Laughter
Ochieng	Born during the daytime
Ode	One born along the road

Odinakachukwu	In God's hands
Odinkemere	Have I done anything?
Odion	The first of twins
Ogbo	Companion
Ogbonna	Father's friend
Ogunshoye	Ogun has done well
Ogwanbi	Fortunate
Ojemba	Traveller
Ojo	A child delivered with difficulty
Okechukwu	God's gift
Okera	A likeness to God
Oko	Elder of twins
Okon	Born in the night

Okpara	Shelter
Olabisi	Joy is multiplied
Olamina	This is my wealth
Olaniyi	There's glory in wealth
Olatunde	Honor comes again
Olu	Preeminent
Olubayo	Greatest joy
Olufemi	God loves me
Olujimi	God gave him to me completely
Olusola	God has blessed me
Olutosin	God deserves to be worshipped
Omavi	The highest
Omenuko	Acts at the time of scarcity
Omolara	A child is my companion
Omorede	Prince
Omoruyi	Respect from God
Omotunde	A child comes again
Omwokha	The second of twins
Onuchukwu	God's voice
Onyedinma	Who is good?
Onyewuchi	Who is God?
Osagboro	There is only one god
Osagie	God agrees
Osahar	God hears
Osakwe	If God agrees
Osayaba	God forgives

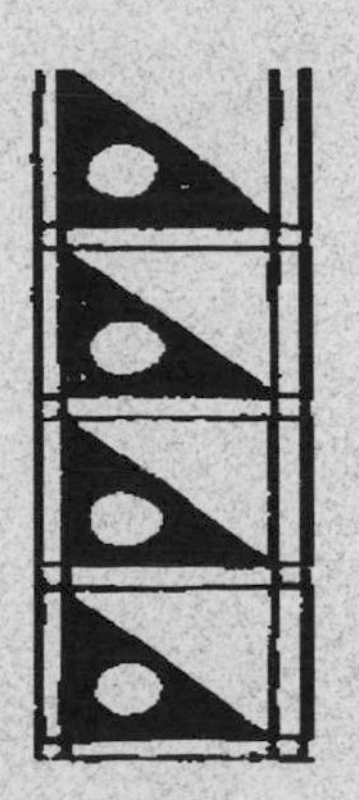

Osayande	God owns the world
Osayimwese	God created me all right
Osaze	Whom God likes; loved by God
Osei	Maker of the great; noble
Oseye	The happy one
Osonduagwuike	One never tires in the struggle or existence
Osuji	Farmer
Othiamba	Born in the afternoon
Othieno	Born in the night
Otuome	He does as he boasts
Owodunni	It is nice to have money
Owusu	The clearer of the way

Paki	Witness
Patire	Where we are
Pili	The second born
Rapuluchukwu	Leave it in God's hands

Rapuokwu	Abstain from quarrels
Rasidi	Good council
Rudo	Love
Sabola	Pepper
Sakidi	Faithful
Sekai	Laugh
Sekani	Laughter
Sekou	Fighter
Sekpuluchi	Praise God
Shermarke	Bringer of good fortune
Sifie	We are dying
Sikukkun	Born on Christmas
Simba	Lion
Simiya	Drought
Simwenyi	One who smiles every time
Sipho	A gift
Siyazini	What do we know?
Sule	Adventurous
Tabansi	Endure patiently
Taiwo	First born of twins
Tasie	Be consoled
Tebogo	Gratitude
Thako	Hip
Thambo	Ground
Tobechukwu	Praise God
Toola	Workman
Tsalani	Good-bye
Tuwile	Death is inevitable

Uba	Wealthy
Ubanwa	Wealth in children
Uchechukwu	God's plan
Udechukwu	God's fame
Udegbulam	May my fame not kill me
Udenwa	Child's fame
Udo	Peace
Ufa	Flower
Ugo	Eagle

Ugochukwu	Eagle of God; illustrious
Ugwunna	Father's fame
Uju	Abundance
Umi	Life
Uwadiegwu	The world is deep
Uwaezuoke	The world is imperfect
Uzoamaka	Road is splendid
Uzoechina	May the road not close
Uzoma	The right way
Uzondu	The way of life
Wamukola	Left-handed
Watende	No revenge
Wemusa	Never satisfied with his wealth

Yao	Born on Thursday
Yawa	Born on Thursday
Yobachi	Pray to God
Zahur	Flower
Zesireo	Elder of twins
Zuberi	Strong

VI. The Northern Region

Female	Meaning
Amira	Queen
Amal	Hopes
Ahlam	Dreams
Abiba	The beloved one
Asa	Life is given
Aisha	Life
Aziza	Dignity
Bakhitah	Fortunate
El-Jamah	Paradise
Fatimah	Daughter of the prophet
Fatia	Daughter of the prophet, one who conquers
Gamer	Moon
Hadiah	Quiet and calm
Kutu	One of twins

Maha	Beautiful eyes
Mbagun	One of twins
Mona	A great surprise
Nadia	Time of promise
Najat	Safe
Neimat	Pleasant
Nun	Brightness
Sara	Gives pleasure
Shaba	Morning has come
Shami	Like the sun
Sit Abua	Her father loves her
Sit al-Banal	Master of girls
Soda	Happiness
Thuraia	Star of my life
Zihur	Flowers are plentiful

Male	**Meaning**
Abdullah	Servant of God
Abdul-rahman	Servent of God merciful
Amal	Hopes
Amin	Honest
Anwar	Shiny

Ali	Highest
Badrak	He has mercy
Bahari	One who sails
Basel	Bravery is his prize
Bilal	Trustworthy
Daw	Light
Dila	Courage
El-Fatih	The conqueror
Farri	A religious man
Fouad	Heart
Habib	Lovely

Hakim	Wise
Haleem	He does not anger
Hamid	Thanking God
Hassiem	Strong
Helal	Like the crescent
Ibrahim	Father
Irwah	Resolution
Jamal	Beauty
Jassiem	Strong
Jumah	Friday
Kareem	Generous
Khamis	Thursday

Malek	Owner
Malik	Owner
Mamoun	Confident
Mohammed	Thankful
Musa	Sharp
Nadir	Rare
Nazim	Wonderful
Omar	Trustful
Rami	He is wise
Saed	Happiness is here
Salah	Good is a reward
Safe el-din	Sword of the religion
Thair	Honest and clean
Yakubu	He is blessed
Yusef	The promise is true